First Studies for the *Oboe*

by William Lindenmuth

1 2 3 4 5 6 7 8 9 0

Visit us on the Web at www.melbay.com — E-mail us at email@melbay.com

PREFACE

This is a series of theoretical and practical studies in a progressive sequence. The material is continuous with no "lesson boundaries." The ability and industry of the pupil will determine the rate of advancement.

The musical compositions are *original* to encourage actual *reading* as opposed to playing *familiar music* by memory. This approach to OBOE playing is melodious, yet designed to insure proper technical development of the beginning Oboist.

THE REED AND ITS CARE

The reed should be moistened (inside and outside the blades) for at least five minutes by immersion in water, or with the player's saliva. It should be slightly open at the tip when properly wet. If the opening is too great, gently squeeze the blades together to correct. Blow from cork end to remove excess moisture.

To play on the reed, open mouth, take a deep breath, place top of reed on dry lower lip, close upper lip on reed, then push reed up and into the mouth to position shown in picture. This procedure should roll the lips into the mouth slightly past the tooth line, forming a firm cushion in which to nest the reed. The upper and lower teeth are parted 5/16" to 7/16" so that muscle tension of the lips, rather than biting action of the jaw, will provide proper playing pressure. The mouth it self is narrowed, forming dimples just outside the corners as in the picture.

Since oboe playing requires a high velocity of wind, pressure must be built up prior to starting a note. Using the whispered syllable "hut", bring tongue tip to reed tip, blocking any flow of air through the reed as abdominal muscles are tensed in preparation to blow. Start the tone by retracting the tongue and releasing a strong stream of air through the reed as if silently pronouncing the word "too." This technique is known as tonguing. Practice this tone production (attack) until instant response is attained; hold each note for two-to-four counts.

After a tone is successfully produced, the next step is to raise and lower the pitch. Using the reed only, slowly play simple melodies by adjusting the reed and lip pressures; i. e. less reed in mouth and less lip pressure will produce lower tones; more reed in mouth and more lip pressure will produce higher tones. It is recommended that the student continue this for one week without the instrument. The range of pitch for this practice should be about F♯ upward to D or E:

When finished playing, blow moisture from reed, wipe blades carefully, and put away, preferably in a reed case. Do not use airtight tubes in which new reeds are sold, as a damp reed stored without ventilation will mildew and be very unpleasant to play. The reed requires extreme care in handling.

Note: Occasionally wipe inside of reed by running an ordinary pipe cleaner through it via the cork end.

The Instrument and Its Care

Most damage to an oboe, by a pupil, is done by careless handling of the instrument while putting it together.

(a)   Assemble "bell" to lower joint taking care to align matching levers.

(b)   Holding the assembly in the right hand and the upper joint in the left, wiggle together carefully so that levers on the lower joint pass under matching levers on the upper joint. (Cork grease should be used sparingly to ease the fit.)

(c)   Twist reed into upper joint until it hits bottom. If cork is too large, carefully sand it down for a proper fit. (A manicurist's emery board is a handy accessory to carry.)

Note: When not playing, remove reed and keep it in its case or in your mouth.

When laying instrument down, keep key side up. This is to keep condensed moisture from running into the the key holes and pads. Keep inside of bore as dry as possible by taking apart and running a turkey feather up into the bore, stroking back and forth with a rotating motion. This applies particularly to the upper joint. Avoid exposing the instrument to extreme temperature changes, as rapid expansion or contraction of wood may result in cracks or checks.

Theory

The music staff consists of five (5) equally spaced lines creating four spaces. The Clef sign locates a specific note from which the others may be located.

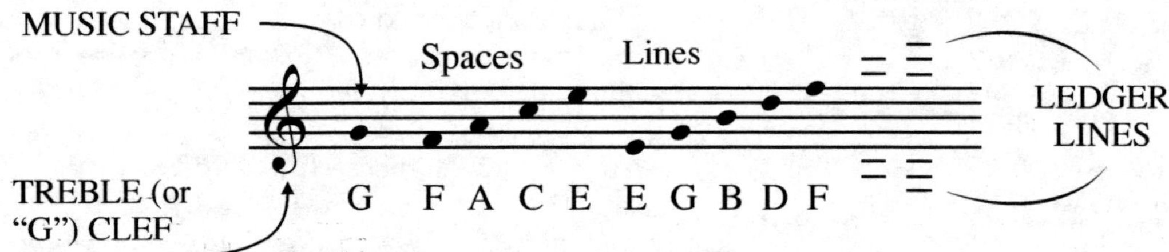

The curl of the old–style capital "G" ( ) locates "G" on the "Treble Clef" staff. Though there are several different *Clefs*, the oboe player is concerned primarily with this one.

"Ledger Lines" extend the musical staff upward or downward. Notes read upward A through G, then starting with A, repeat the sequence over and over (line–space–line–space, etc.)

Relationships

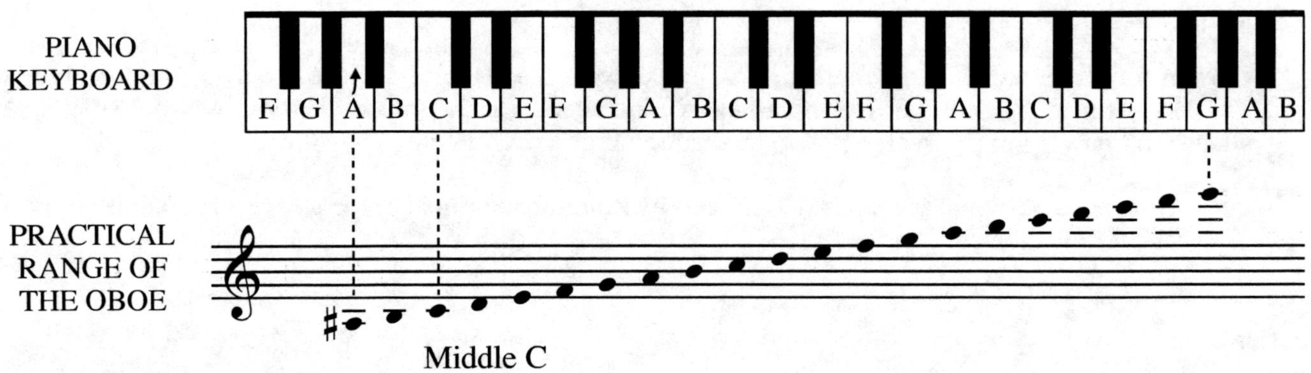

The oboe has a practical chromatic tonal range of A♯ (B♭) below middle C through high G as shown on page 4.

There are twelve equal–pitch intervals in an octave (C to C; D to D; B♭ to B♭; etc.) These are known as Chromatic intervals or half–steps, and can be easily traced on the piano keyboard by taking each key in order, whether it be black or white.

The white notes are generally considered to be Naturals; the black notes are called Flats (♭) or Sharps (♯). The black note between C and D, for example, may be called C♯ or D♭. The symbol ♯ (sharp) means a half–step higher; the symbol ♭ (flat) means a half–step lower. The symbol ♮ (natural) indicates an unaltered note, or a white key. All written notes are considered to be natural unless altered by key signature or accidental.

The Major Scale

The Major scale is Diatonic. This means that it is composed of eight (8) notes in a specified sequence of Whole–Tone and Half–Tone intervals. The Major scale, commonly known as the "DO–RE–MI–FA–SOL–LA–TI–DO" scale, is constructed as follows:

ALL MAJOR SCALES ARE CONSTRUCTED IN THIS FASHION:	(Ascending)	
	Do to Re	= whole step (2 half steps)
	Re to Mi	= whole step
	Mi to Fa	= half step
	Fa to Sol	= whole step
	Sol to La	= whole step
	La to Ti	= whole step
	Ti to Do	= half step

C MAJOR SCALE

Syllable	DO	RE	MI	FA	SOL	LA	TI	DO	
Note Name	C	D	E	F	G	A	B	C	
Degree of Scale	1	2	3	4	5	6	7	8	(1)

G MAJOR SCALE
If we should select "G" as a key–center, or "DO", the scale is:

	DO	RE	MI	FA	SOL	LA	TI	DO	
	G	A	B	C	D	E	F♯	G	
	1	2	3	4	5	6	7	8	(1)

The "F" is "sharped" to meet the interval conditions of a major scale. The "sharp" placed on the "F" line demands that all F's be sharped unless shown otherwise.

B♭ MAJOR SCALE
Given B♭ as a key–center, the scale is written:

	DO	RE	MI	FA	SOL	LA	TI	DO	
	B♭	C	D	E♭	F	G	A	B♭	
	1	2	3	4	5	6	7	8	(1)

Here the B's and E's are "flatted" to comply with the interval rules. The number of flats (♭) or sharps (♯) following the Clef sign (𝄞) indicates the key–center, and is called the "KEY SIGNATURE".

The normal sequence of sharps or flats occuring in key signatures remains unchanged regardless of how many are needed:

It is suggested that the student demonstrate his understanding of MAJOR Scale construction by writing scales of D Major, E♭ Major, A Major, A♭ Major, and B Major. Leave space for KEY SIGNATURE, adding the sharps (or flats) in correct order after their need is correctly established.

NOTES AND EQUIVALENT RESTS:

Ratio of Note Values

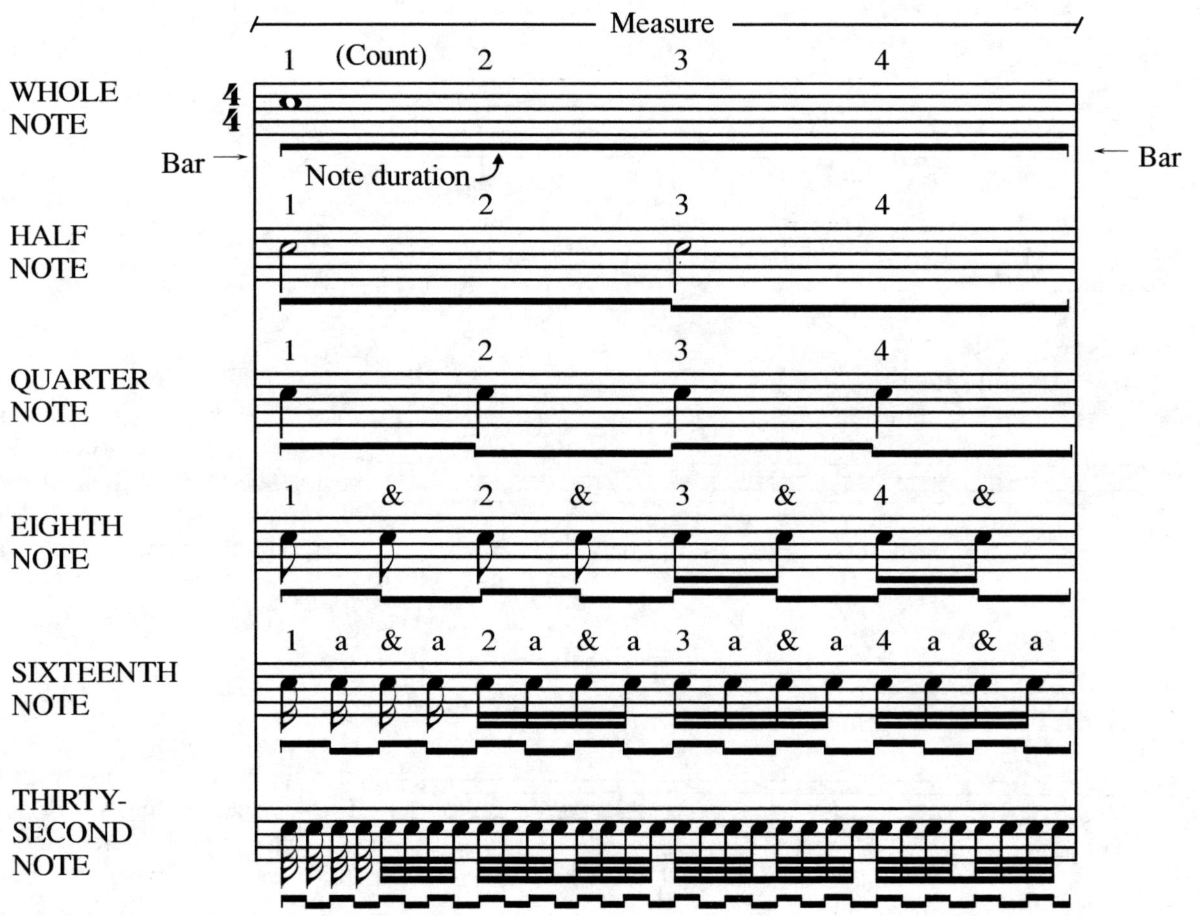

Time Signatures

There are several common <u>TIME SIGNATURES</u> such as: $\frac{2}{4}$; $\frac{3}{4}$; $\frac{4}{4}$; $\frac{6}{8}$ etc.

The lower number represents the value of the TIME–UNIT being used. The upper number represents the sum of these units needed to fill a complete measure.

Examples:

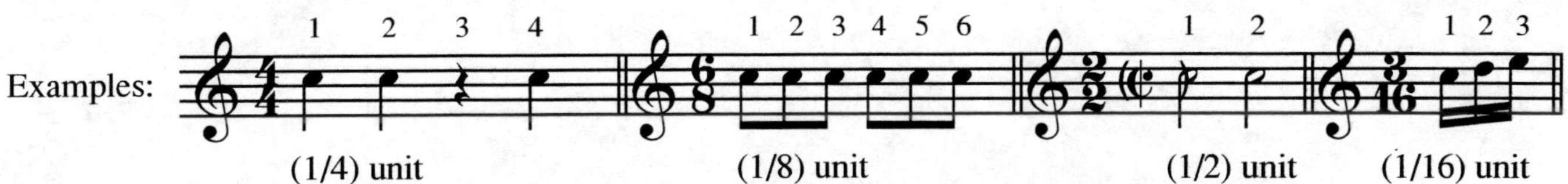

The Tie

The *TIE* is an indication to connect notes of the same pitch into one longer note whose time–length equals the sum of all notes so tied.

Example:

The Dot

The <u>DOT</u> (.) following a note, rest, or another dot, increases the time value of the symbol immediately preceding it by one–half.

Example:

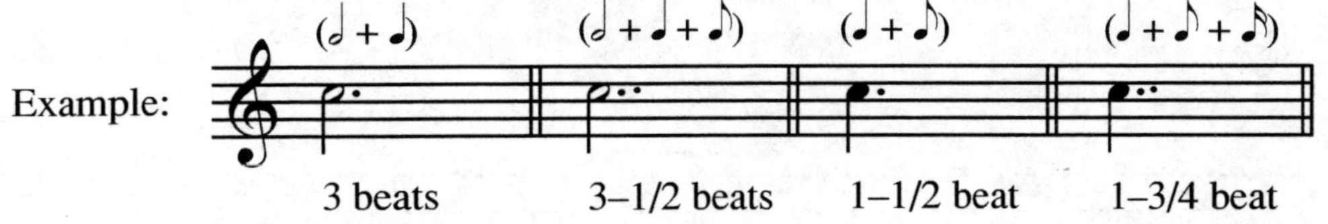

Scheme of Oboe Key System

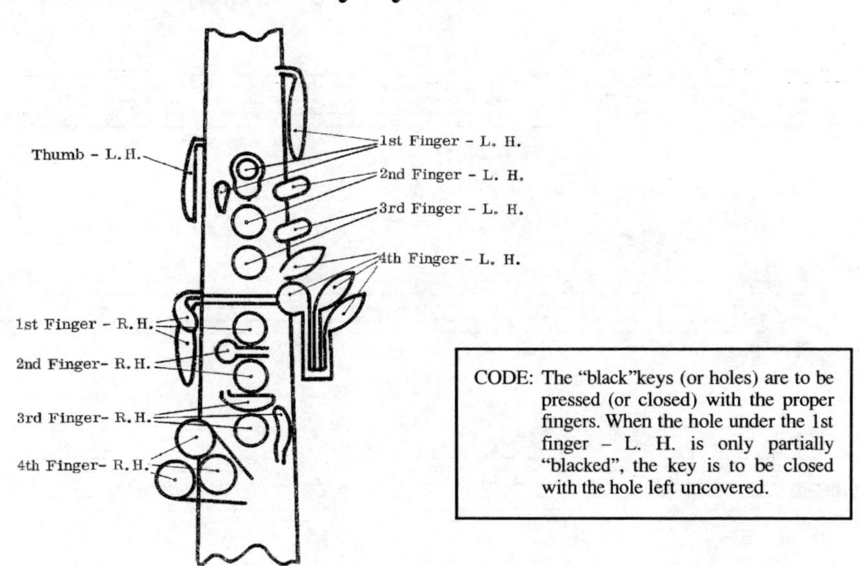

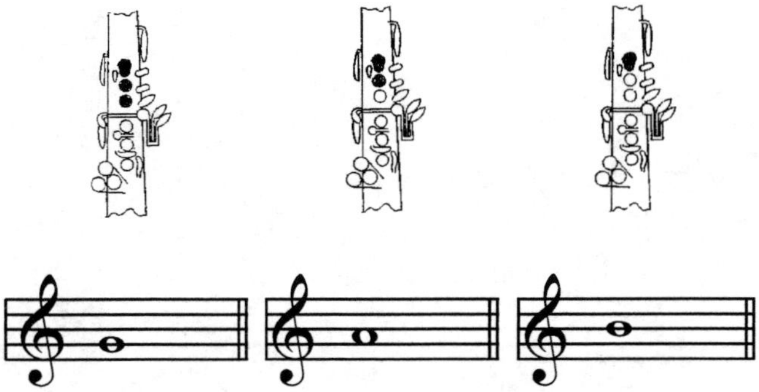

START EACH NOTE
WITH THE TONGUE.

(count)

1. G   Rest

2. A

3. B

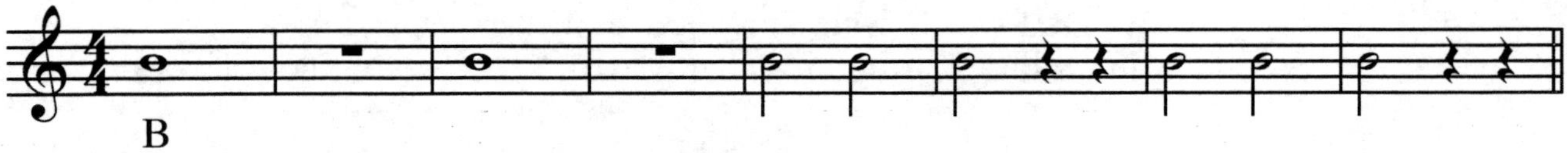

Adam

4.

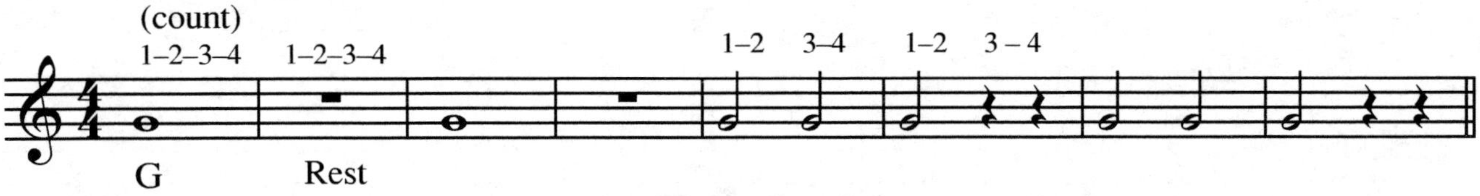

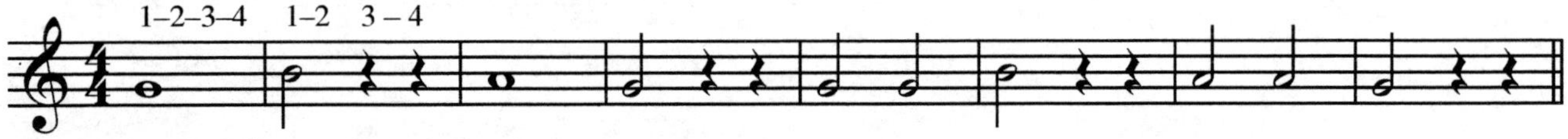

Eve

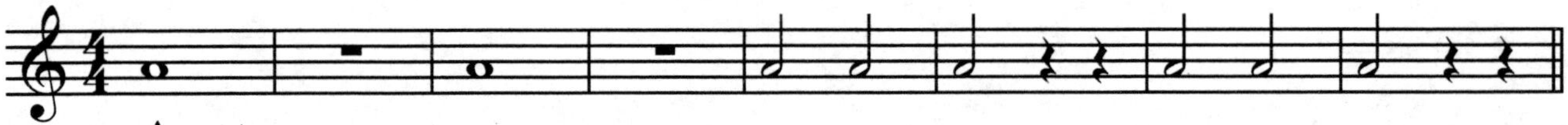

5. Rest

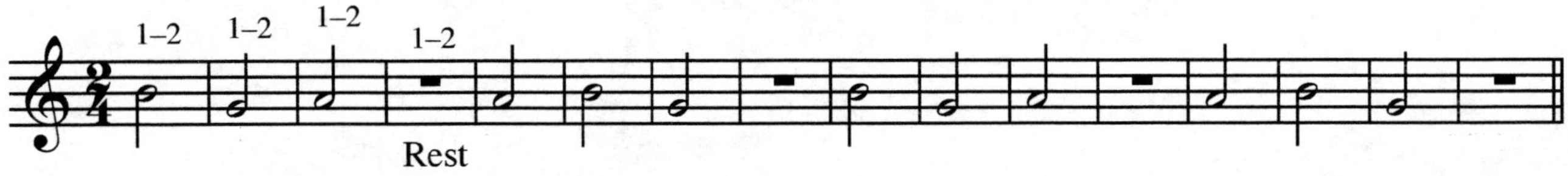

Cain

6.

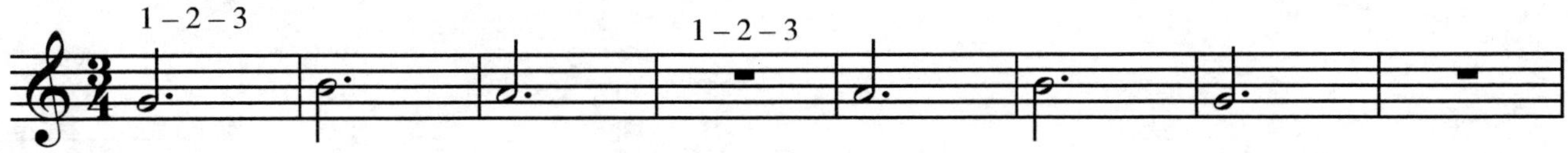

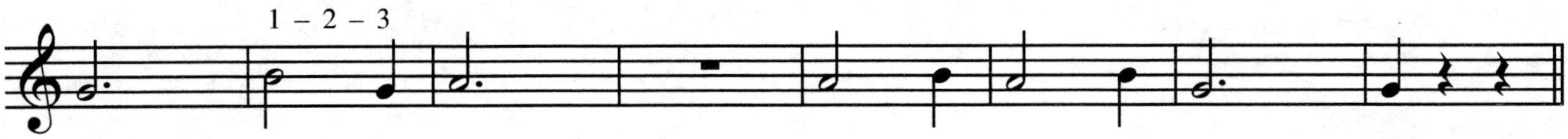

Abel

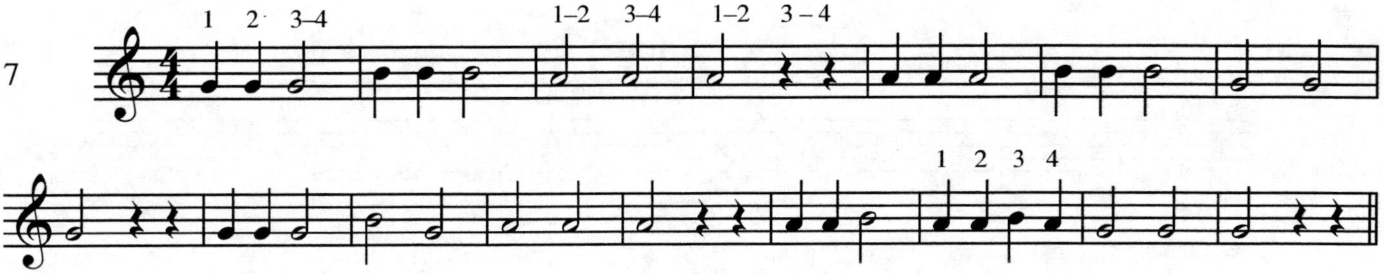

Seth

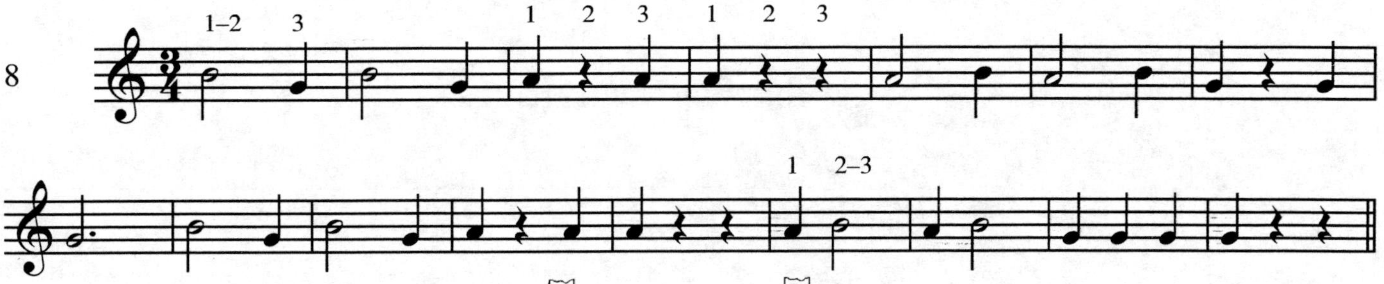

NEW
NOTES

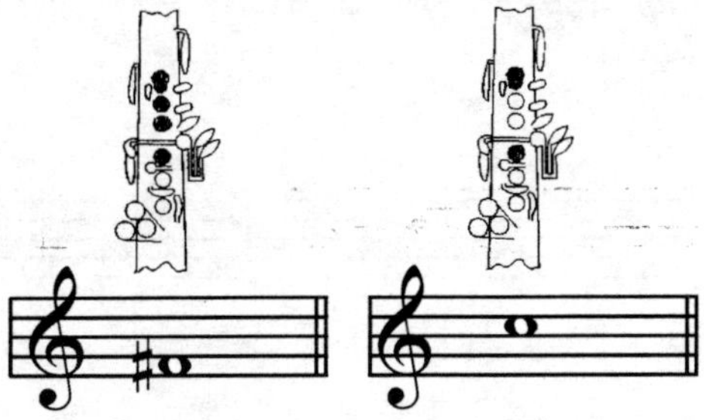

GIVE EACH NOTE FULL TIME VALUE.

slowly

Theme

The standard sign for taking a breath is the COMMA (**,**)

Song

Melody with Variations

NEW NOTES

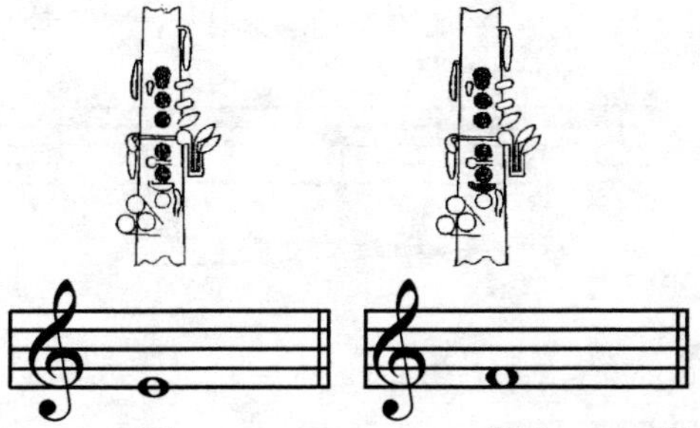

E   F (natural)

The Slur

The Slur is an indication to play two or more notes in a smooth, *legato*, style without interruption by tongue or breath.

Example

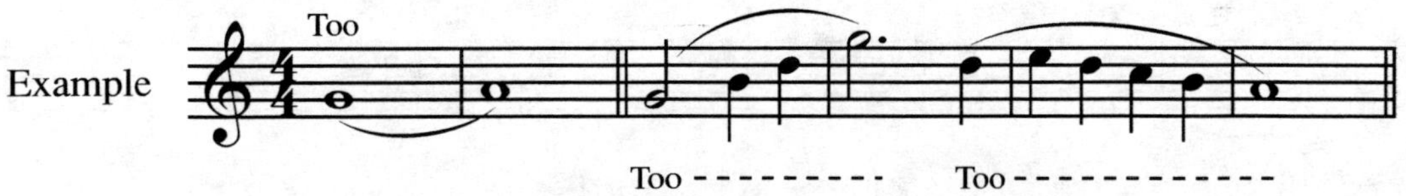

Theme with Variations

17

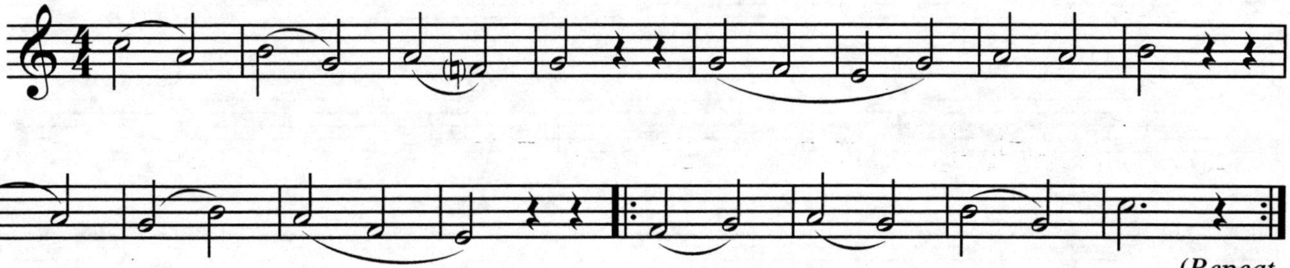

(*Repeat from opposite sign*)

VARIATION I

18

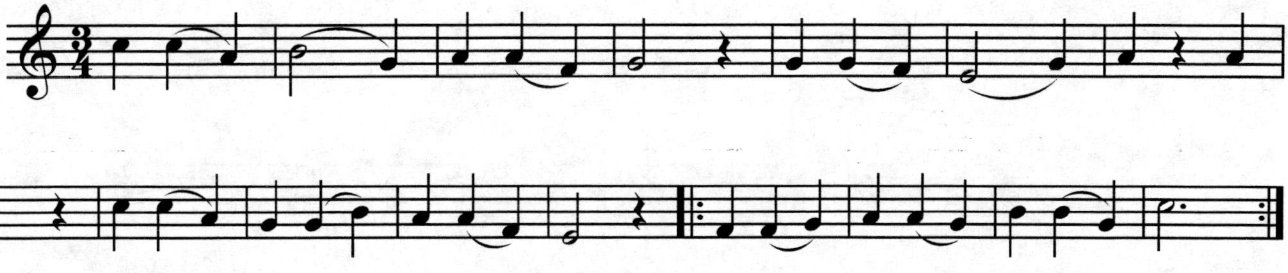

VARIATION II

19

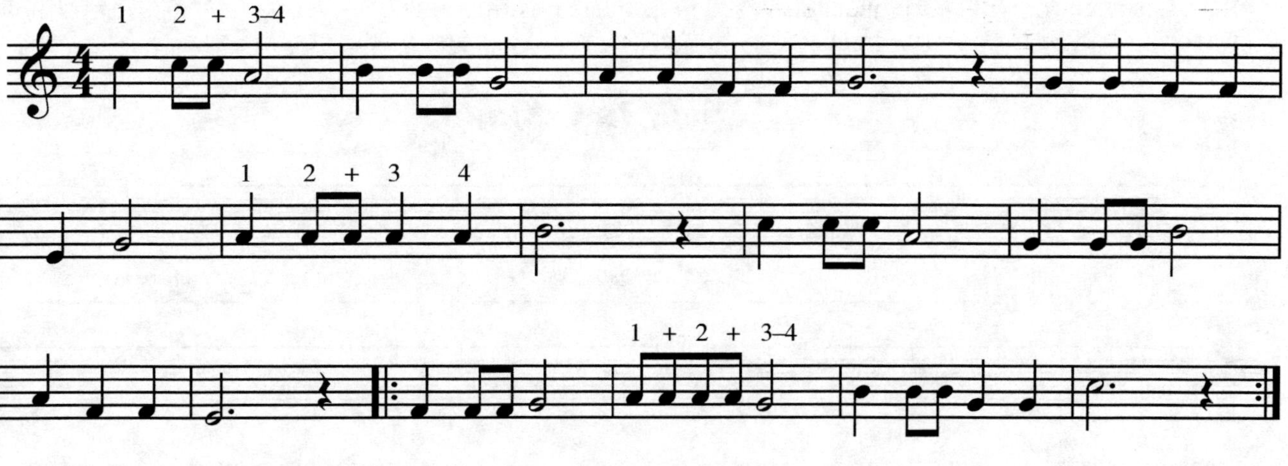

The ACCENT symbol (>) demands a strong attack.

Example

ff

VARIATION III

20

Exercise in Thirds

(Key of G Major)

21

— 3rd —

tie

NEW
NOTES

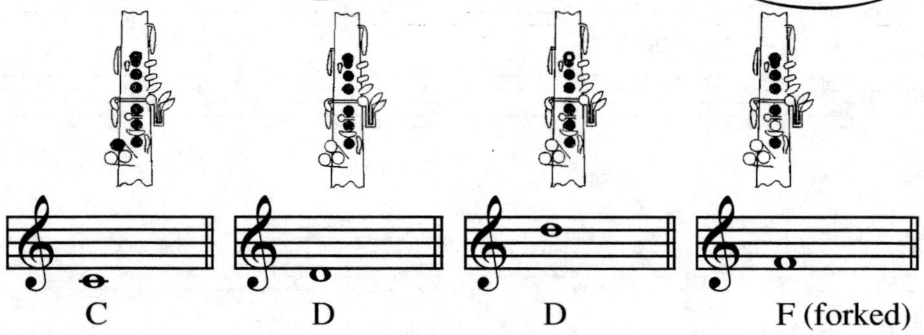

C   D   D   F (forked)

The "Forked" F fingering has been devised to provide another way to produced "F" when the 3rd finger, R.H. has been (or will be immediately) used in its basic position: that of covering the "D" Key (or hole). This fingering will be temporarily indicated by an asterisk (*) over or under the note.

Song in C Major

22

1.

2.

(These measures are played 1st time thru only)   (These measures are played 2nd time thru)

Common Dynamic Terms

SYMBOL	ITALIAN	ENGLISH
pp	*pianissimo*	very soft
p	*piano*	soft
mp	*mezzo piano*	medium soft
mf	*mezzo forte*	medium loud
f	*forte*	loud
ff	*fortissimo*	very loud
< *cres.*	*crescendo*	increase sound
> *decr.*	*decrescendo*	decrease sound

Tempo Indicators

1. very slow

   Largo
   Lento
   Adagio

2. slow

   Larghetto
   Adagietto

3. moderately slow

   Andante
   Andantino

4. moderate

   Moderato

5. moderately fast

   Allegretto
   Allegro

6. very fast

   Vivo
   Vivace
   Presto

Changes of Tempo

increase speed gradually	decrease speed gradually
accelerando *stringendo*	*rallentando* *ritardando*

faster immediately	slower immediately
più mosso *veloce*	*ritenuto* *meno mosso*

Country Dance

Allegretto

23

Seconds

Allegro

24

Etude

Andante

25

* **

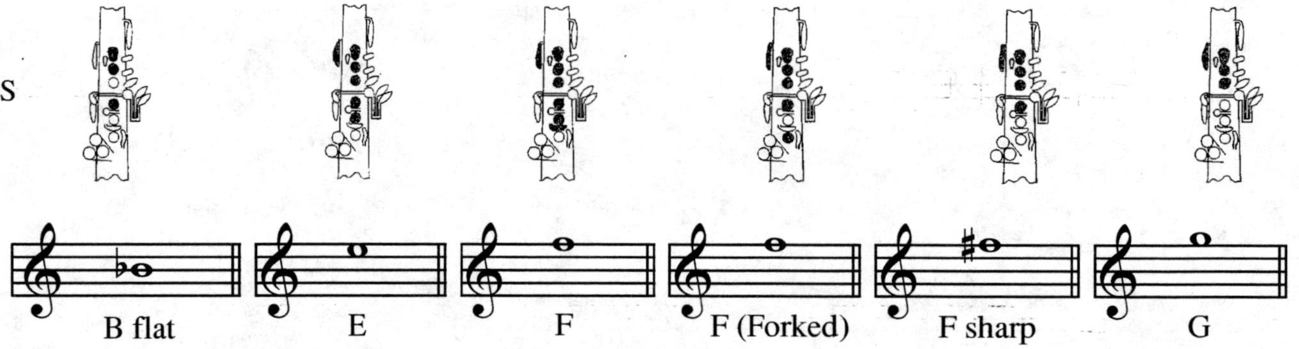

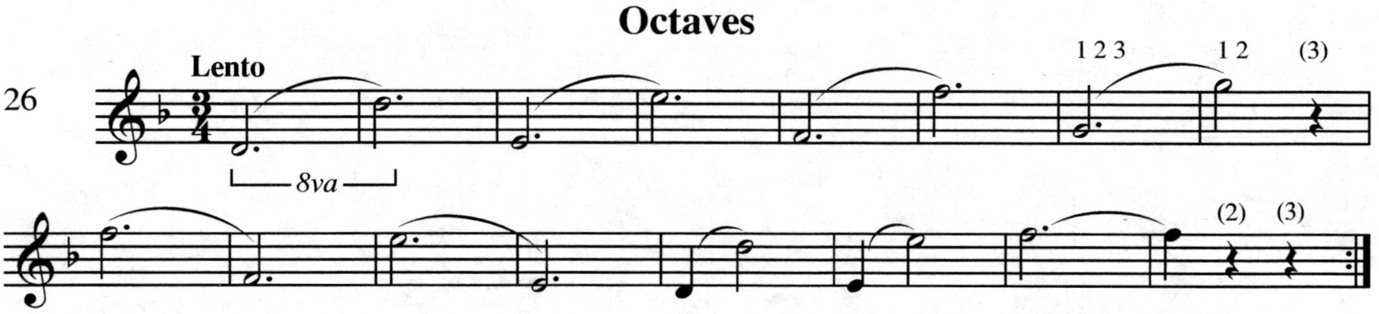

Note: The E, F, F#, & G in the second register are fingered like those of the lower register, except for the addition of the thumb octave key.

Octaves

Lento

26

1 2 3   1 2   (3)

8va

(2)   (3)

'F' Scale Waltz

27

Moderato
f

Lullaby

28

Andante
mf – mp
(1x) (2x)

Skips and Flips

29

Allegro
f
*
*
*

The Dotted Quarter Note (♩.)

1 – 2 + 3 – 4 +
Played ---------------- Written

Other Examples
1 – 2 (+) 3–4 (+)
1 +2 3 +4
(1)+2 (3)+4
(1) + (2) + (3)+4

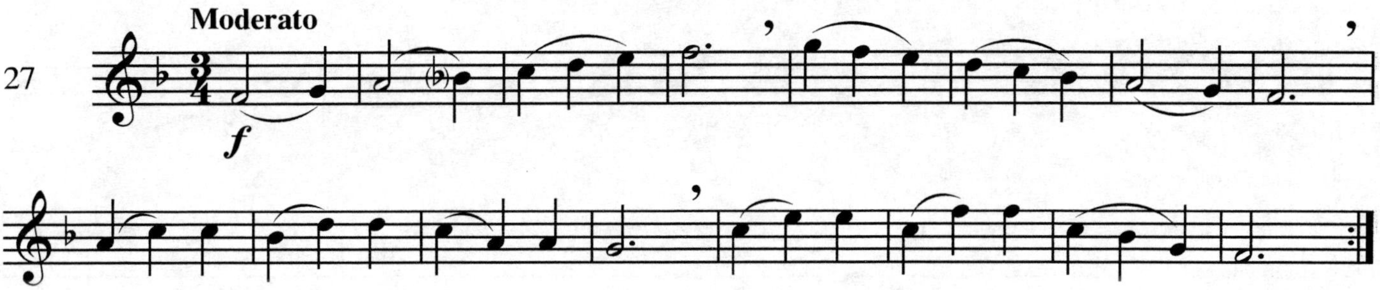

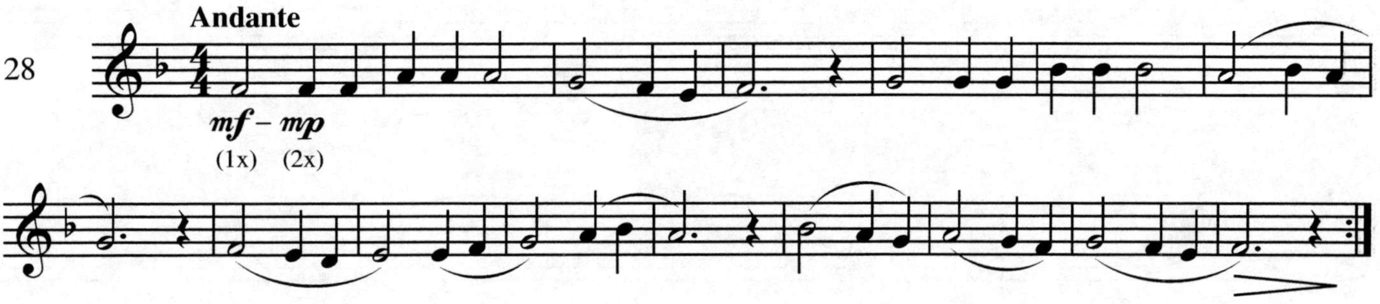

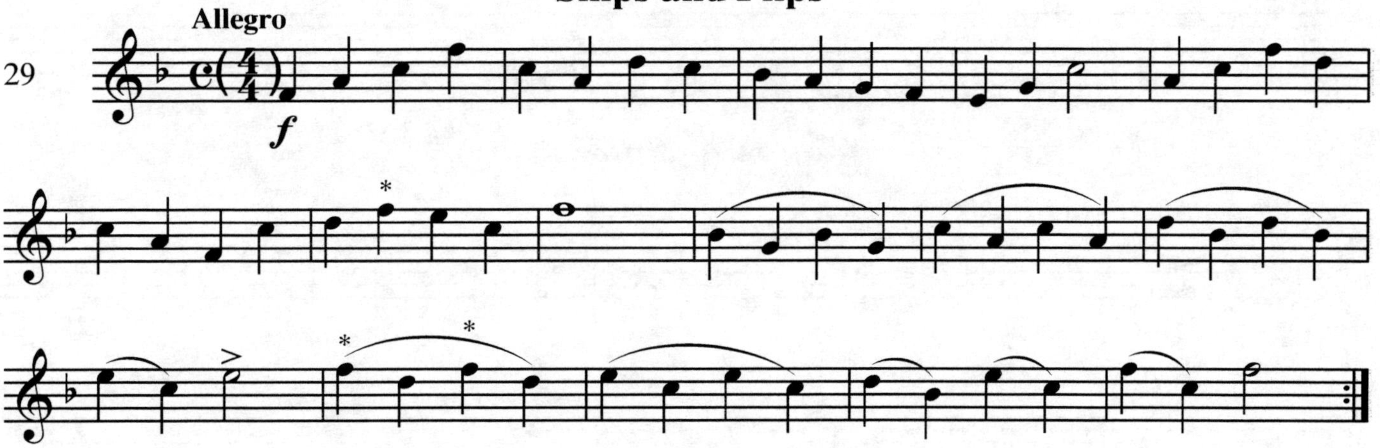

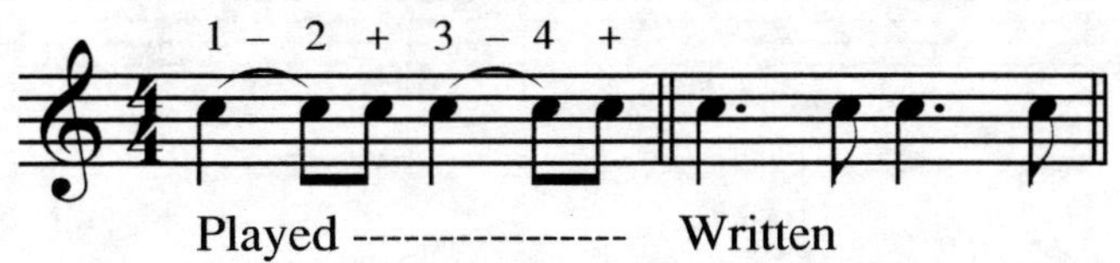

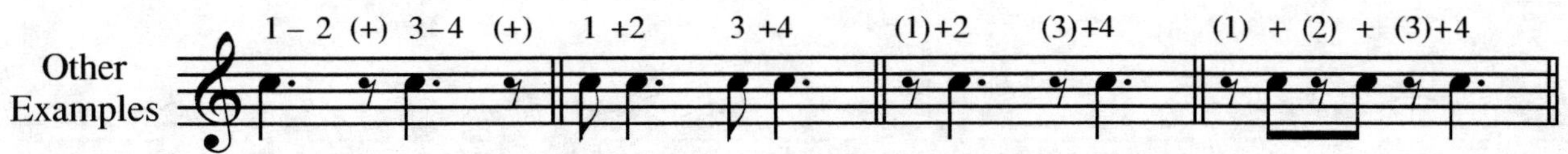

Signal Fire

Signal Fire
Moderato
1–2   + 3–4
30
f
'G' Waltz
Allegro
31
mf 1   2–3 +   1–2–3
1–2   + 3
1   2–3 +
Whistling
Allegretto
32
f

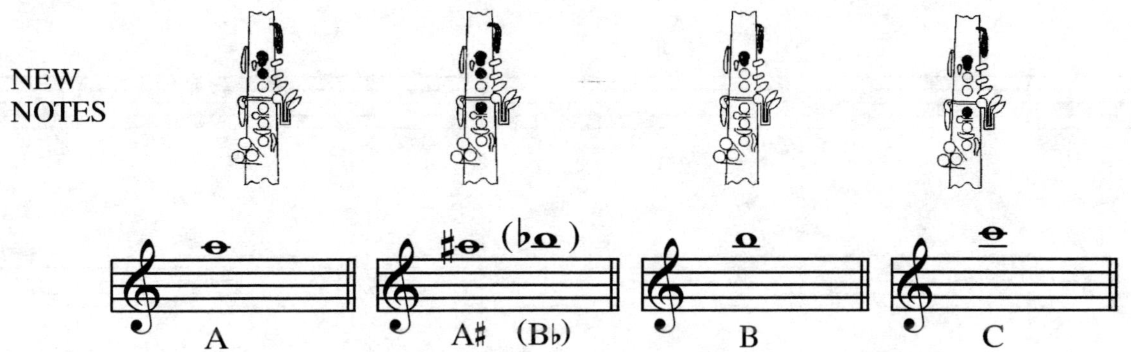

Note: These notes require the use of octave key #2 (see master chart) played with 2nd joint of left hand index finger. The L.H. thumb may remain on octave key #1 if prior note requires it.

Fourths

33

Smiles

Moderato

34

Count one–two
two–two
three–two
four–two   Then Repeat

Over the Fence

The COME SOPRA is an indication to repeat notes or measures. These are typical examples:

Waltzing with Willie

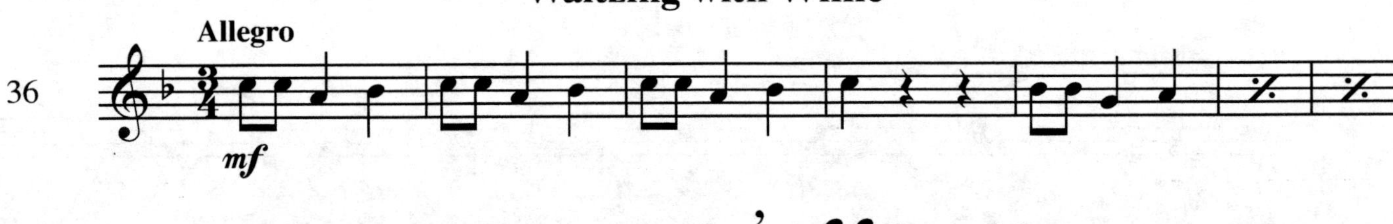

Sonus

THE FERMATA ( ) indicates a <u>hold</u> of indefinite length. The normal pulse of the music <u>slows</u> or <u>halts</u> while this liberty is exercised. It should be used in <u>good taste</u>.

Exercise in Thirds

Sail Away

Strata–One

Strata–Two
41
f
Day–Break March
Allegro
42
mf
ff
Rough and Ready
Tempo di Marcia
43
mf
f
ff
20

Accidentals

In any specific key, there may occur a pitch–alteration (♭, ♯, or ♮) not common to that key. This change is valid for the register (level) indicated <u>only</u>, and lasts for the rest of the measure, unless changed again. In the following measure, all such altered notes revert to their original key with the exception of TIES.

The ♭'s, ♯'s or ♮'s used in this temporary manner are called ACCIDENTALS.

Skip–Jack

Moderato
46
mf
f
mf
f
Up–Town
Allegro
47
mf
Down–Town
Allegro
47A
mf
Pearly Gates
Moderato
48
mf

B♭ Scale and Chord

F Scale and Chord

C Scale and Chord

G Scale and Chord

D Scale and Chord

The Pet Parade

Turn–About March

NEW
NOTES
Clouds
Andante
57
p
f
p
f
simile
f
p
simile
Evening Song
Andante
58
mp
f
B♭ Major Scale
59
c
f
25

Staccato

A *Staccato* note is played in a short, crisp, detached style; usually with more accent than for normal playing. Since the note is shortened, a rest is used to fill the *time–space* required. *Staccato* is indicated by a dot (.) or point (❜) over or under the note. The degree of *Staccato* will be influenced by the music being performed.

NOTE: The "Forked F" is no longer starred. It is now up to the pupil to foresee its application.

Birds on the Roof

Allegro

62

The Robot

Moderato

63

RULE: A note with a DASH (♩̄) is to receive <u>maximum</u> time value. This device is often used to insure contrast; especially when intermixed with staccato notes.

Summer Night

Slowly

64

Jigolet

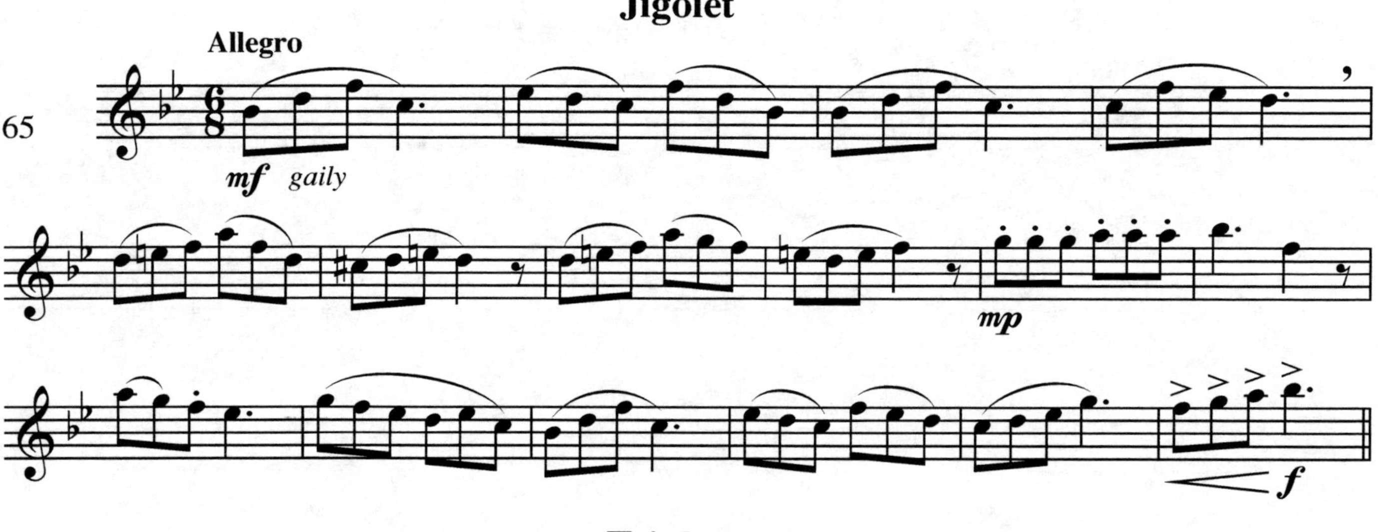

Triplets

Three Time–Value units, when crowded into the same Time–Space normally used by Two such units, are called TRIPLETS. The figure "3" is generally used for identification.

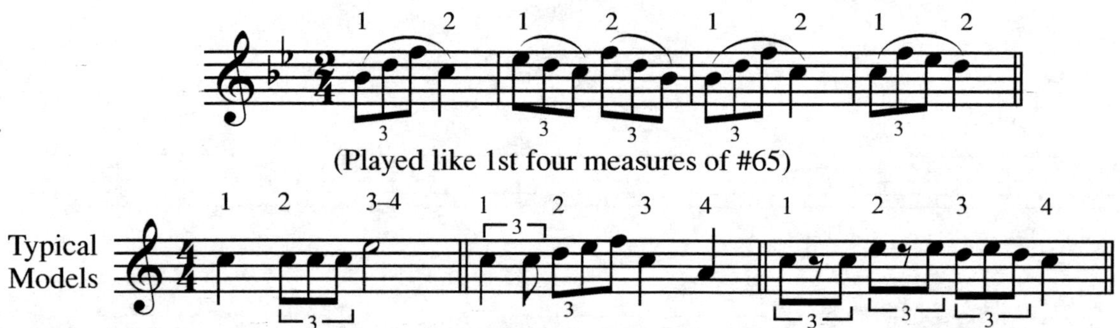

In the song "Row Row Row Your Boat", this phrase is a perfect example of triplets:

Count: 1 – a – ly   2 – a – ly   3 – a – ly   4 – a – ly

(Words) Mer – ri – ly Mer – ri – ly   Mer – ri – ly Mer – ri – ly

Coronation March

The Robust Men

67

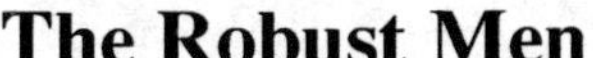

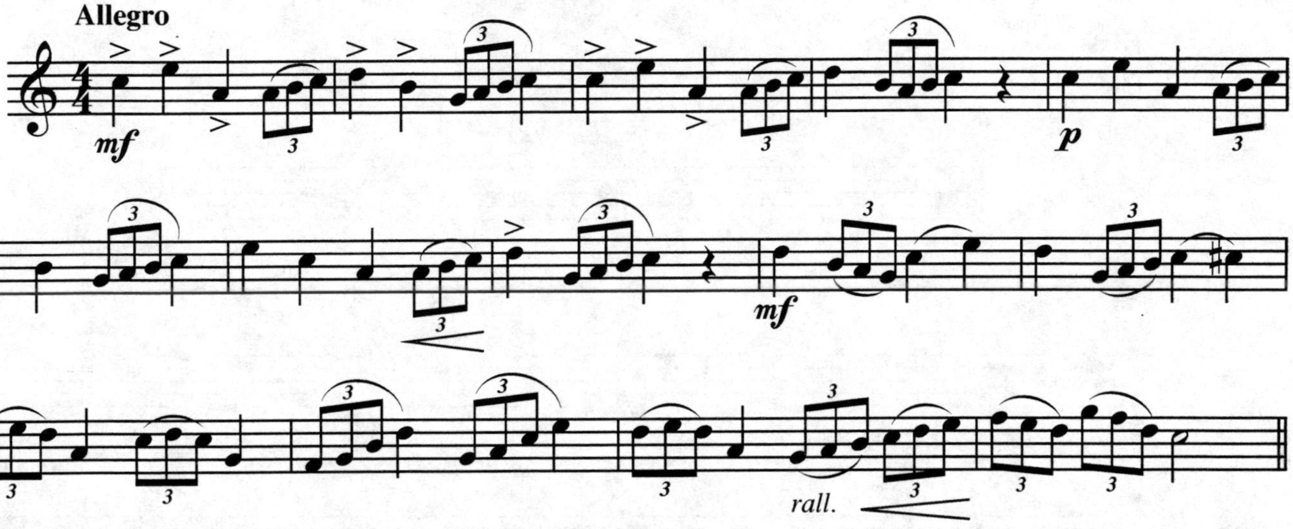

Meditation

68

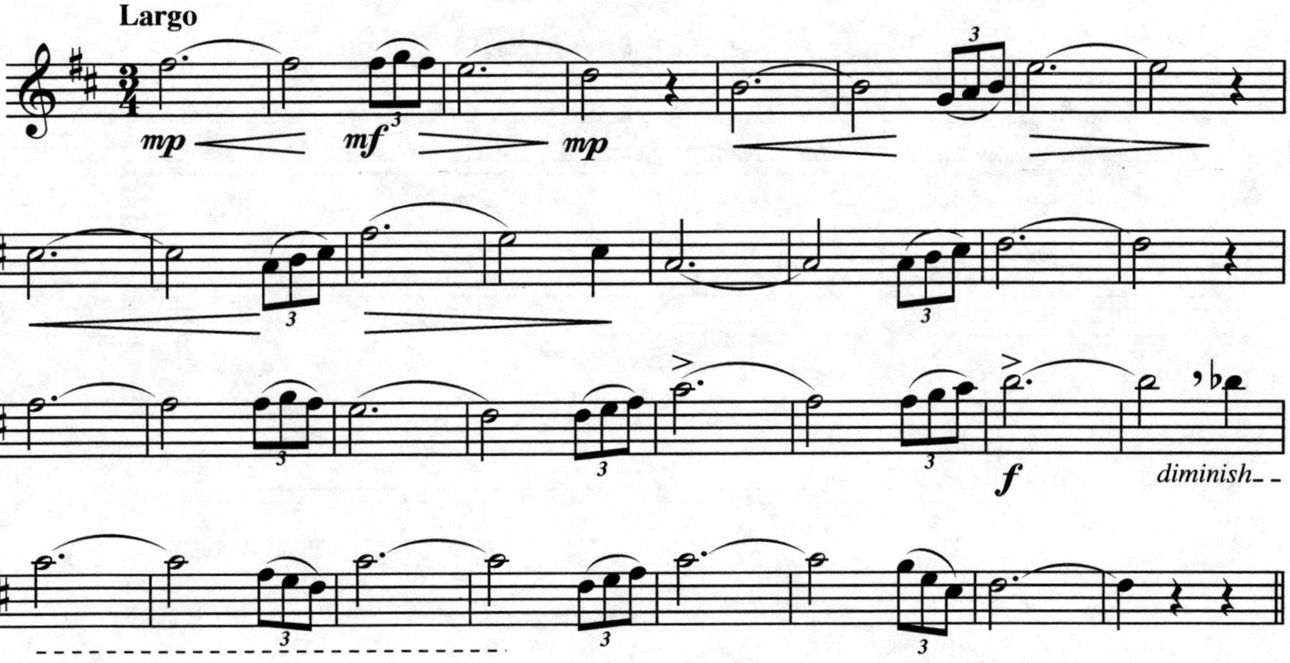

Rolling Along

69

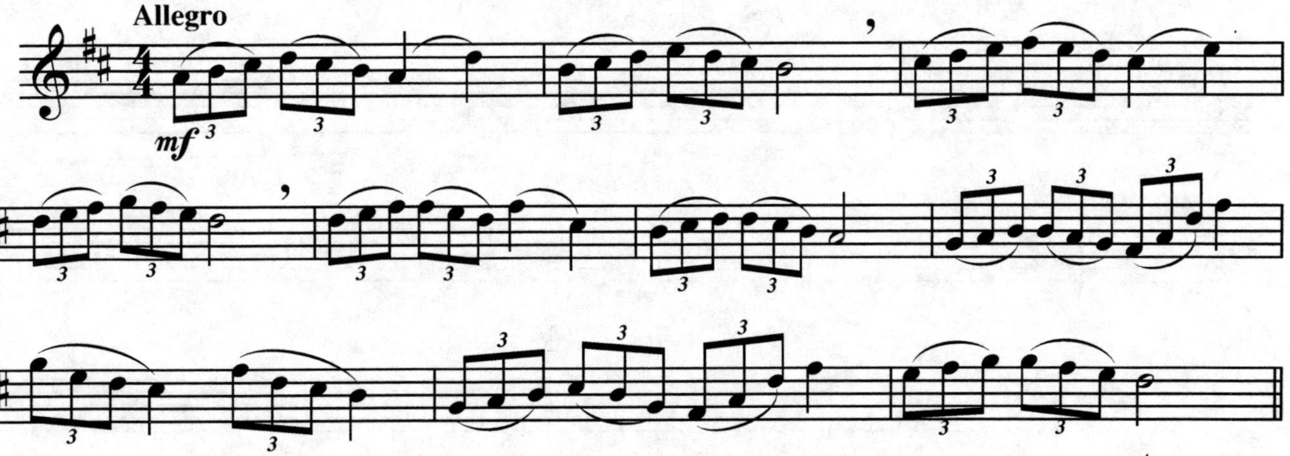

NEW
NOTES
Scenario
Slowly
70
mf
3
3
3
3
3
3
3
Key of A Major
Briskly
71
mp
mf
p
"Alla Breve"
Written:
Played:
C or (2/2)
2/4
Ballad
Moderato
72
mf
f
mf

Astronaut's March

Octaves

Octaves
Lento
76
mf
Pulsation
Moderato
77
mf
ff
Frolic
Allegretto
78
f
1.
2.
Tone Control
Slowly
79
mf
mf
mf
mf
mf
mf
mf
mf

Homework

Homework
Moderate
80
f
Poise
Slowly
81
mf
Progress
Allegro
82
mf
f
ff
f
mf
mp
ff

Night Song

Night Song
Andante
83
mf
Duet
Play both lines alternately.
84
mf
Enduro
Lento
85
mp
mf
simile
mf
Song–In–Six
Allegro
86
mf

Duet
Moderato
mf
f
87
FINGERING
REMINDERS
Key of E♭ Major
88
1.
2.

Syncopation

SYNCOPATION refers to notes* starting on the weak beats of rhythm and holding through the strong beats.

Rag–Time

Banjo Baby, Cake Walk

Waves

Tango

Tango
92
mf
f
Chord Study
93
"A"
"D"
"G"
"C"
"F"
"B♭"
"E♭"
(♮)
rall.
Quiet Night
94
Moderato
mp
f

Common Fingerings
(By half steps)

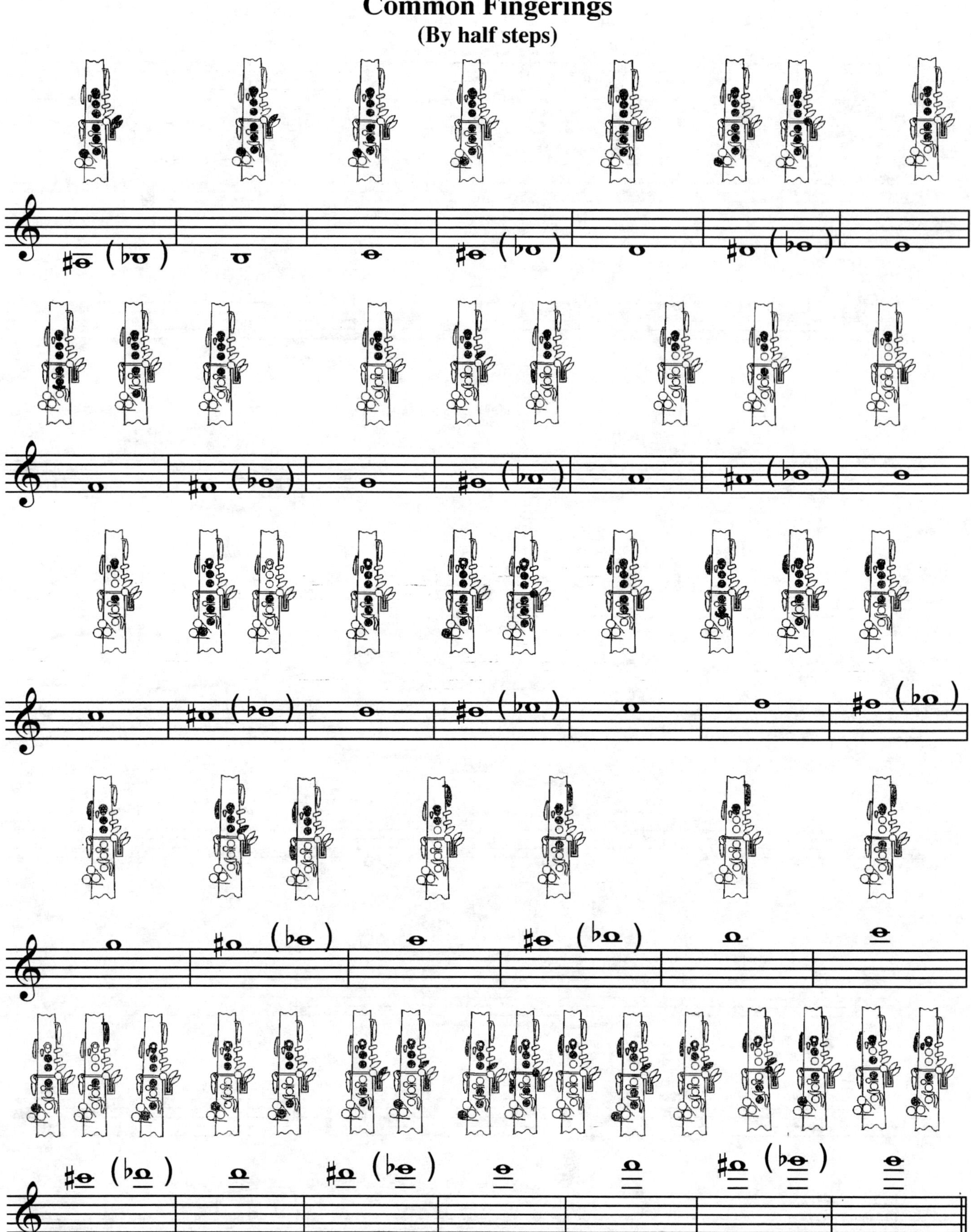

Chromatic Waltz

Exercise in Chromatics

Chromatic Scale expressed in E♭ Major

Chromatic Scale expressed in A♭ Major

9/8 time is usually conducted in "3", or THREE BEATS TO THE MEASURE. The Player must sub-divide each beat into 3 equal parts as though to play 3-1/8th note triplets to each conducted bar. **6/8** time, when fast as in a march or jig is similarly conducted in "2"; **12/8** in "4".

Shadow Land

* Double flat ♭♭ (Note lowered by two semi-tones)

** Double sharp ✗ (Note raised by two semi-tones)

mp
f
mp
mf
f
Exercise in Thirds
101
Reverie
In "4"
1   2   3   4 – 5   6   7 – 8 – 9   10–11–12
102

Vibrato

The oboe is a solo instrument featured in a large variety of lyrical music. Since the "singing style" is desirable, the oboist requires a fluent knowledge of the use of *vibrato* (pulse). The most practical method of producing vibrato is with a pulsating breath as though saying "whoo-whoo-whoo". It is important that the speed and degree of undulations be under the performer's strict control.

The shortest acceptable *vibrato* is of two-pulse duration; if a note passes too quickly to permit two pulses, no *vibrato* is used. In addition to being good technical exercises in several keys, the following etudes offer a practical means to acquire the mechanics of *vibrato*. In these studies the eighth (♪) note is to be the equal of a pulse unit. Only notes of at least quarter (♩) value should be pulsed. The eighth note rhythms as arranged here set the tempo for the pulse on the longer notes. The slow tempo indications should be accompanied by an exaggerated pulse. When the high tempo is finally attained, a smooth *vibrato* should result.

In the ultimate performance the oboist does not necessarily time his vibrato to any rhythmic unit of the music being played. The *vibrato*, at this point, should be a natural, smooth embellishment used to enhance the overall musical performance.

Five Finger Frolic

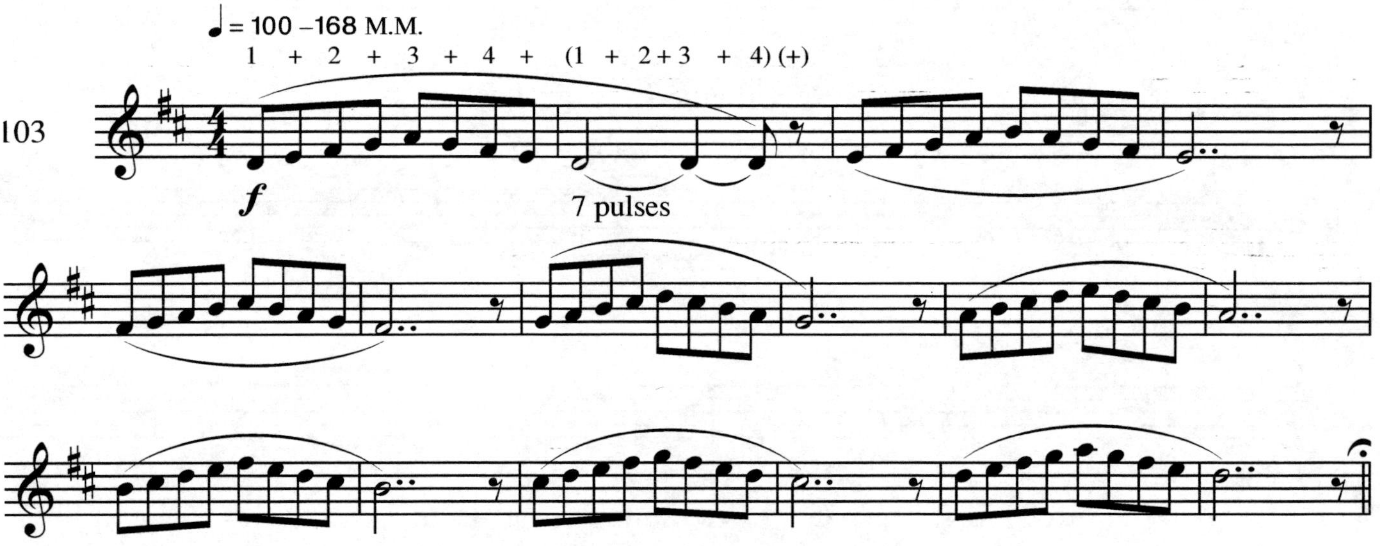

Head–on

Triplet Pulse

109
♩. = 66 – 112 M. M.
f (3)
(4)
mf
f
f
(2)
mf
mp
mf
f

Diatonic Thirds

110
♩. = 66 – 112 M. M.
(3)
(0)
(7)

111
♩ = 100 – 168 M. M.
f 2 pulses
(5)
(5)

Pearls for the Sultan's Daughter

Technique

Play the repeated measure three (3) times in each of the following phrases:

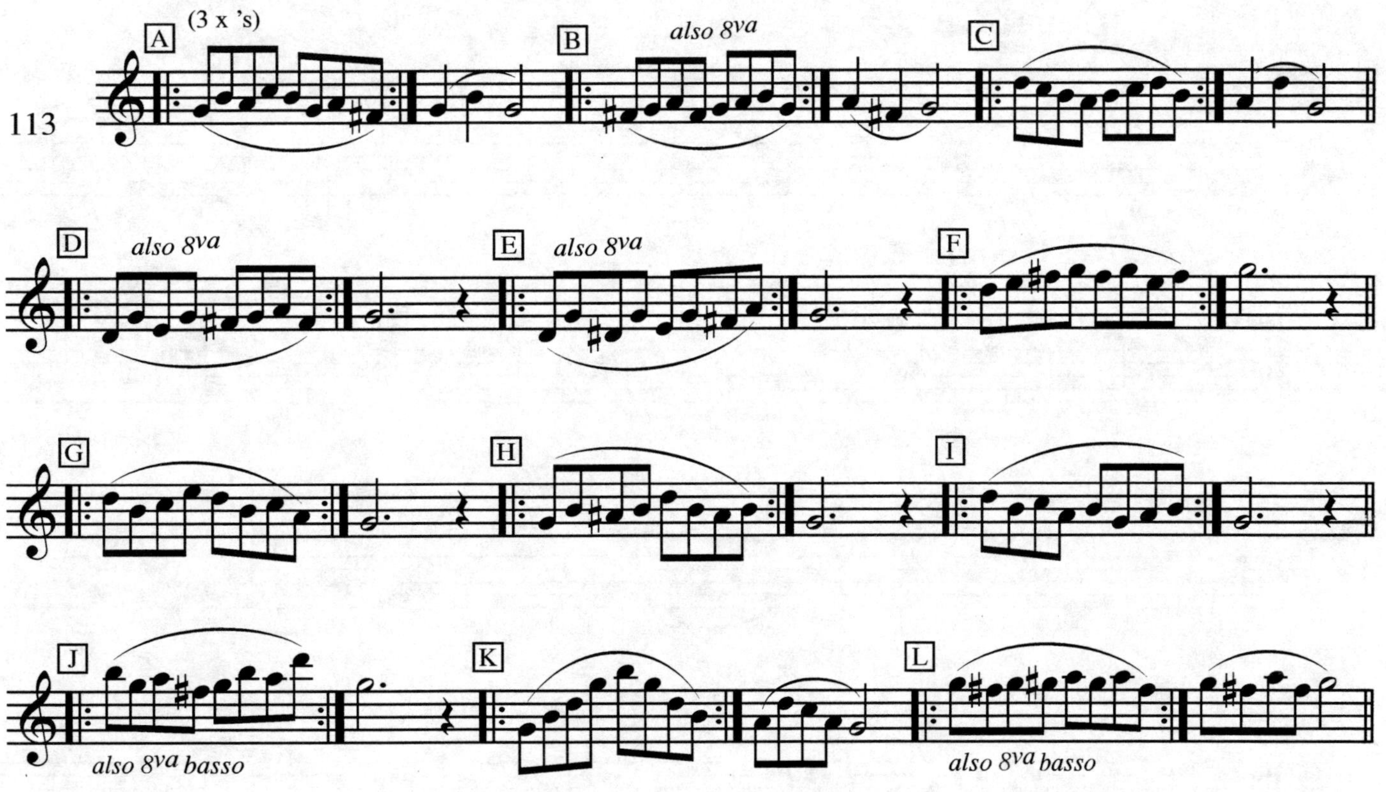

114
(3 x 's)
A
B
> > >
C
D
E
F
also 8va
G
H
I
J
K
L
also 8va
115
(3 x 's)
A
>
B
C
D
E
^ ^ ^
F
G
H
also 8va
I
J
K
L

116

A
(3 x 's)
B
C
D
E
F
G
H
also 8va
I
J
K
also 8va basso
L
also 8va

117

A
(3 x 's)
B
C
D
E
F
G
H
I
J
K
also 8va basso
L

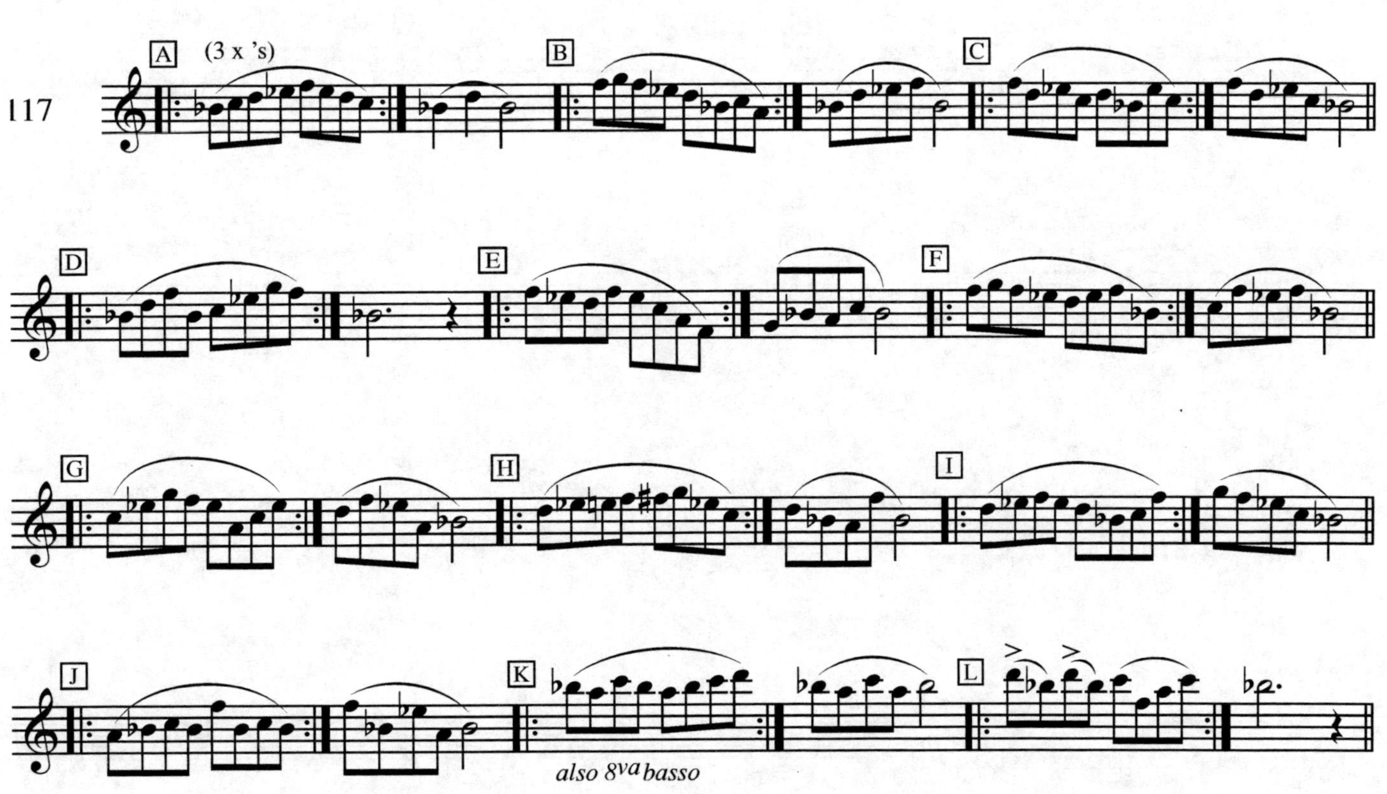

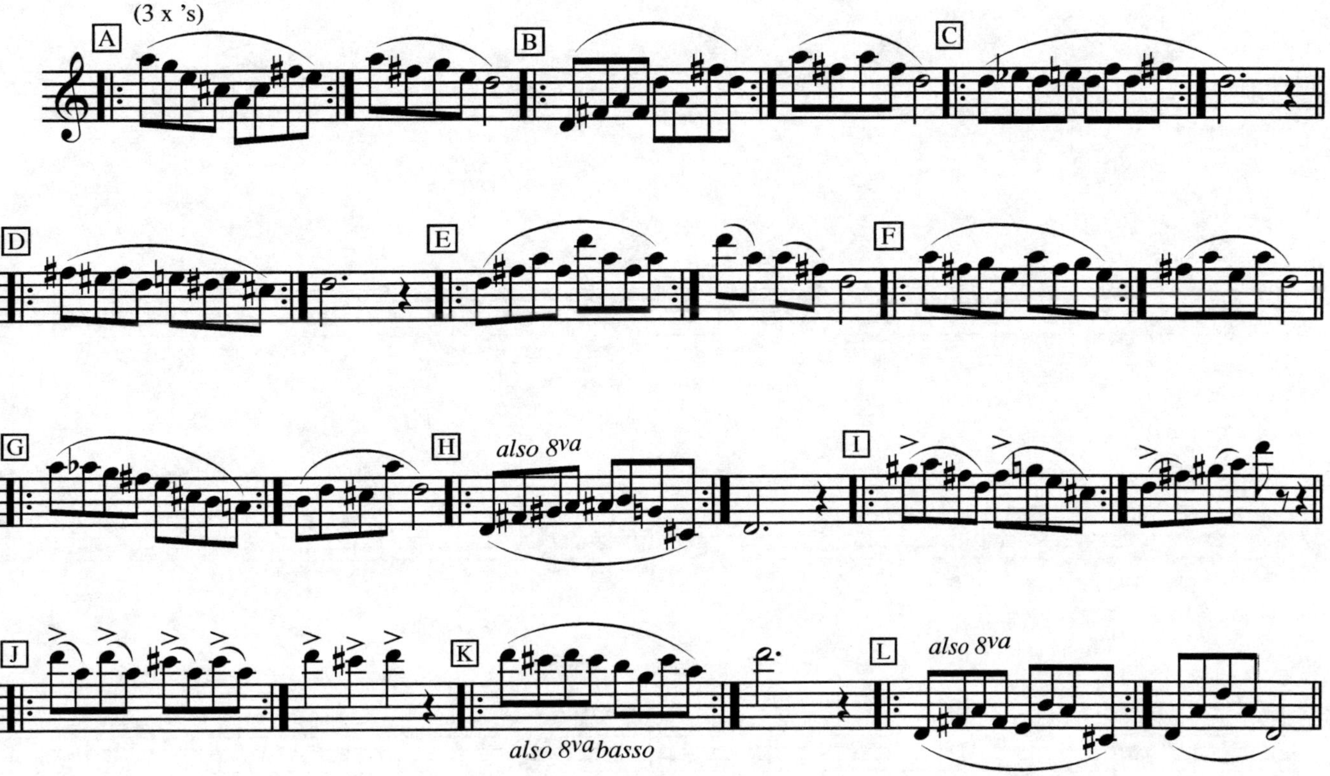

118
(3 x 's)
A   B   C
D also 8va   E   F
G also 8va   H   I
J   K also 8va   L also 8va
119
(3 x 's)
A   B   C
D   E also 8va   F also 8va
G   H   I
J   K   L
also 8va basso